The 5 Key Success Factors

A Powerful System For Total Business Success

By E.W. 'Buck' Lawrimore

A POWERFUL SYSTEM FOR TOTAL BUSINESS SUCCESS

The 5 Key Success Factors:
A Powerful System For Total Business Success

Copyright 2011 by E. W. "Buck" Lawrimore

Lawrimore Communications Inc.
1320 Fillmore Ave., Suite 312
Charlotte NC 28203 USA
www.Lawrimore.com

All rights reserved. No part of this book may be reproduced, stored in a retrieval system, or transmitted in any form or media, except for brief quotations for reviews, without the prior permission of the author.

Cataloging-In-Publication data is on file with the U.S. Library of Congress.

ISBN **978-1-257-15654-2**

Printed in the United States of America

First Edition 2011

Table of Contents

Introduction: What Are The Enduring Success Factors? 5

    THE MOST IMPORTANT SUCCESS FACTORS THAT WORK 5

    DEFINITION OF SUCCESS FACTORS 6

    SUCCESS FACTORS AND LIVING SYSTEMS 7

    THE STAR MODEL OF SUCCESS FACTORS 8

Key Success Factor No. 1: Strategy 9

    CONCENTRATING YOUR RESOURCES – AN ANCIENT CONCEPT 9

    STRATEGY VS. STRATEGIC PLANNING 9

    THE FUNDAMENTALS OF STRATEGIC PLANNING 10

    IMPORTANCE OF THE DEFINING ELEMENT 11

    CLARIFYING CORE VALUES 12

    CREATING A CHALLENGING MISSION 12

    SETTING A FEW KEY GOALS 13

    DEVELOPING A STRATEGY FOR EACH GOAL 14

    THE LIVING SYSTEMS PERSPECTIVE 15

    THE IMPORTANCE OF ABUNDANT COMMUNICATION 16

    SYSTEMS THINKING FOR BEST RESULTS 17

    THE SIGNIFICANCE OF LEARNING 18

    ADAPTING TO THE CHANGING ENVIRONMENT 18

    INTERRELATIONSHIPS WITH OTHER SUCCESS FACTORS 19

Key Success Factor No. 2: People 21

    PEOPLE, PART 2: WHAT THE WORLD'S GREATEST MANAGERS DO DIFFERENTLY 25

    PART 3: A LIVING SYSTEMS APPROACH TO PEOPLE AS A KEY SUCCESS FACTOR 27

Key Success Factor No. 3: Marketing 28

    MARKETING FOR THE SMALL BUSINESS 28

    OTHER APPROACHES TO MARKETING 35

Key Success Factor No. 4: Operations
. . . Or, What You Do All Day 42

Key Success Factor No. 5: Finances and Facilities 46

Chapter 7: Integrating the 5 Key Success Factors With A Total Success System™ 50

Introduction: What Are The Enduring Success Factors?

The Most Important Success Factors That Work

"What are the most important success factors that enable one organization to succeed while others stumble or fail?"

Since the early 1980s and the publication of *In Search of Excellence* by Tom Peters and Bob Waterman, thousands of authors, professors and consultants - including me - have attempted to answer that question. What makes this so challenging is to identify success factors that:

- Work effectively for a wide variety of organizations, not just Fortune 500 companies with huge budgets, but for any small business, nonprofit or government organizations
- Really make a difference in improving tangible results, such as improved income and profits, customer loyalty and retention, employee satisfaction and performance, quality and operations improvement
- Will stand the test of time – not be the fad of the moment or the flavor of the month, and therefore...
- Are grounded in concrete reality and lasting truths, not just subjective ideas.

In this book, I will share with you what I have discovered through decades of research and experience with many organizations, to be the most important, reliable, powerful success factors of all time—and especially effective in the challenging 21st Century. I work as a consultant every day with organizations of all kinds, mostly small to mid-size businesses and government-funded departments or institutions. My aim is to help increase their success in terms of increasing sales or operating income, enhancing brand awareness and image, improving performance and quality, getting more out of employees through enlightened management and personal understanding. The powerful success factors described in this book can be a tremendous asset for you as well.

Definition of Success Factors

We might define "success factor" as "one of several elements that consistently cause or produce success in any business or organization." Implicit in this definition is the important awareness that *one* success factor by itself will NOT cause full success, any more than pure sugar will make a cake. Instead, just as with a good recipe, success factors must be combined in the right combinations to yield successful results.

After studying many, many lists of success factors by different authors and "experts," including my own real-world experience, I was finally able to cut to the core of why certain success factors are essential for any business or organization. The reason is, quite simply, because they reflect the very nature of what a business or service organization is and does. Here's how this works:

- Every organization is composed of **people** (employees, associates, managers etc.) and **things** (offices, equipment, money etc.).
- Every organization engages in **activities** which are **internal** and **external**.
- Every organization has a **focus** or **purpose** (like making money or serving the public).

But it is not just the **existence** of these factors that ensures success. They **exist** in all organizations, by definition. It is the **management** of these factors, how they are used, that ensures success. To turn organizational factors like those above into success factors, we must use more business-like language. Keep in mind the very simple, realistic foundation of these success factors as described above, and they will be like your anchor in the storm or a house built on rock. First I will identify the 5 Key Success Factors, then explain in more detail how you need to use them or manage them to achieve greater success. Each of these factor names is **symbolic** – no one word captures all the dimensions of each factor, but the words I have chosen are simple, widely used, and easy to understand. Just remember not to oversimplify as you think about and use them.

1. **People** – Your employees and personnel within the business, or as this function is often called, human resources, including training and learning
2. **Operations** – Your internal activities, what your people do all day

3. **Marketing** – Your external activities, much more than selling to customers, as we will discuss
4. **Finances** – Not just your money but your equipment, furnishings, facilities and all the other "things" your company owns or leases
5. **Strategy** – Maintaining a distinctive focus and purpose, including internal elements such as core values, and external elements such as market strategy and strategic planning

Success Factors and Living Systems

Now it is extremely important to understand that these 5 Key Success Factors are not a hierarchy – I could have put any one of them first. I put strategy first because it gives purpose to all the others, but that reflects my personal preferences. One problem with writing is that it is linear – one word follows another, so lists are a natural way of writing. But lists do not exist in the real world. Instead, the real world is composed of what are called **living systems**. So just as important as the **identity** of the 5 Key Success Factors is the **relationships** between them – they are **interactive** and **interdependent**.

For example your body is a living system. Take away your heart and blood vessels, or your brains and nerves, or your bones, or your internal organs, and you are no longer living and you're no longer a complete system. Just as the human body is an incredible system of millions of interactive parts, all essential for survival, an organization is even more incredible because it is composed of *multiple* humans, with people inside the organization interacting with customers and others outside the organization. Understanding how all these different systems are connected and interdependent in larger systems is called the **systems perspective** or **systems thinking**, and is tremendously important for achieving and sustaining success in the 21st Century. That's because the Internet, the global economy, cell phones, television and other forms of communication interconnect all of us as individuals and organizations, interactively and interdependently. You can't understand anything in isolation. It must be viewed as part of a living system, and a system of systems, that is truly global today. Or if you want to think about the sun and stars, it's truly *universal*.

A POWERFUL SYSTEM FOR TOTAL BUSINESS SUCCESS

The Star Model of Success Factors

From the systems perspective, we can view the 5 Key Success Factors through this "star model," which shows each success factor in relationship with every other success factor:

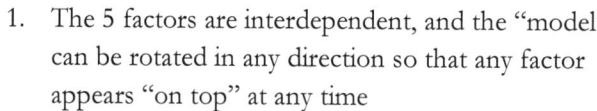

What does this model suggest? Three important things:

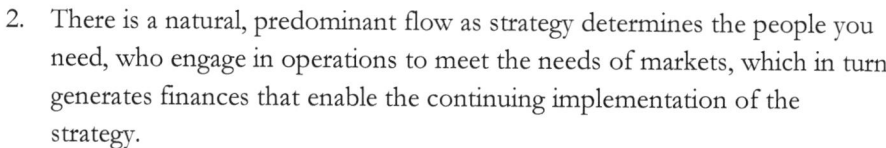

1. The 5 factors are interdependent, and the "model" can be rotated in any direction so that any factor appears "on top" at any time
2. There is a natural, predominant flow as strategy determines the people you need, who engage in operations to meet the needs of markets, which in turn generates finances that enable the continuing implementation of the strategy.
3. But "flow" is not just circular. Every factor is necessarily interconnected to every other factor, not just individually but collectively, meaning that there are actually 5 X 4 = 20 interrelationships to consider at any time. (Technically the total is more like 5X4X3X2 = 120, but we let's keep it simple for now.)

In fact one of the biggest causes of failure in business and government is viewing people and situations as isolated objects, without understanding how everything is connected. I find it quite helpful, when I get into situations that are complicated and lose my bearings, to fall back on the 5 Key Success Factors, which can be very useful tools for getting a handle on almost any problem or challenge. That's because they are rooted and grounded in concrete reality – people and things, internal and external activities, purpose or focus, as explained earlier.

Again, it's not the factors themselves that ensure success, but how you use them. So let's turn now to each factor in more detail, keeping in mind that in a living system, everything is interdependent, and the sequence is somewhat arbitary.

Key Success Factor No. 1: Strategy

Concentrating Your Resources – An Ancient Concept

The 5 Key Success Factors I have identified are so interdependent that it is almost impossible to say one is more important than others, but I have chosen to begin this series with the Success Factor that makes all the others hang together: **Strategy**.

Strategy has both external and internal dimensions. Like the Greek word on which it is based (*strategos* = general), strategy involves both a plan to win on the "battlefield" (the marketplace) and skill in managing "troops" (people, organization, processes etc.). In fact, drawing further on this military metaphor, the essence of strategy can be defined as:

Concentrating resources on your greatest opportunities.

Generals win battles by concentrating armed forces at the point where the enemy is weakest and most unsuspecting. Athletic games are won by finding weak spots in the opponent's defensive line and breaking through. And the game of business is won by finding spots (niches) in the marketplace where (a) you can build on your strengths, and (b) competition is weakest.

Very few businesses engage in conscious, deliberate strategy. It is far more common to start a business based on what the founder(s) know how to do from previous jobs, and continue on as long as that works. However, most small businesses fail, and one of the main reasons is that they do not use strategy. They just do what they know how to do. When the money runs out or the debts run up, they fold.

Strategy vs. Strategic Planning

Probably the most common form of strategy is *strategic planning*. Done right, strategic planning is extremely valuable, and we cover the key steps in that process below. However, *strategic planning* is like deciding what route you will take to drive 800 miles to a vacation spot. **Strategy** is like figuring out what to do in real time as you drive down the highway, encountering opportunities like long stretches of open road, and problems like traffic jams, accidents, detours and speed traps.

Some people would call this type of real-time activity "tactics" instead of strategy. But the point I am making is that truly effective strategy *involves continuous adaptation to the changing environment*, whether that environment is a battlefield, a football field, a marketplace, a highway or the natural environment. I include the natural environment example as a reminder that this definition of strategy is totally consistent with the living-system view of reality and success, which will be mentioned repeatedly in this book. In the natural world, a living system like an ant colony or a human tribe must adapt to their changing natural environment in order to survive and thrive. No food? No water? Go somewhere else. Adapt or die.

First we are going to look at strategy from the more traditional standpoint of strategic planning. Then we will look at strategy from the new perspective of dynamic living systems.

The Fundamentals Of Strategic Planning

1. Develop a shared vision. A vision is a "word picture" of the desired future state for an organization, typically stated in the present tense as if it were already achieved. Although some people have made light of "the vision thing," when properly understood, it is *the main thing*. As the saying goes, "The main thing is to make the main thing the main thing." It's easy to get sidetracked. The best vision statement:

- Represents the thoughts, feelings and aspirations of the entire organization, not just leaders.
- Very concisely, in a paragraph, paints a word picture of the desired future situation.
- Is strongly influenced by market realities, especially what customers value most.
- Challenges the organization to stretch and work hard but is by no means impossible.
- Distinguishes the organization from its competition in a way that is real and achievable.

Importance of the Defining Element

This final element, what I call the *defining* element, is most often missing from well-intended vision statements that sound so much alike. For example, "We are the leader in our markets by providing our customers with superior products and services, our employees with meaningful work and competitive compensation, and our shareholders with an exceptional return on investment." Yeah, yeah, isn't everybody.

To be truly defining, a vision must say, in effect, we will be at the top of this particular mountain or niche. It's what marketers call *positioning*. For example: "We are the leading health-care architect in the Southeast specializing in wellness centers." Or this: "We are the leading manufacturer of lithium compounds and products in the United States." Or maybe just: "We are the best pizza restaurant on the block." In other words, define your expertise and then narrow your scope to an area small enough that you can actually dominate it. That is truly defining your vision, and because it is realistic and achievable, your people will find it believable.

Because a vision statement must be concise and compelling, it is best developed by a small group, typically the management team, then circulated internally to all personnel, encouraging feedback and refinement. Some companies print their vision statement on a business card and give everyone a copy. Others simply publish the whole strategic plan.

Most vision statements have all the enduring power of a movie or advertisement. Once it is seen, it is soon forgotten. To make your vision statement last, to make it truly meaningful, you and other top executives must walk the talk, use it in meetings and conversations, employ it in making group decisions, refer to it in internal communication, and repeat, repeat, repeat. If you are not prepared to nurture and sustain a vital vision statement, don't start one in the first place. Neglected vision statements lead to cynicism and skepticism. It's hard for people to take it seriously over time, and especially later on when you want to update it or try again.

Clarifying Core Values

2. Clarify core values – Values are guides for action, reflecting the deeply held beliefs and value systems of the leaders and people of the organization. The highly successful book "Built To Last: What Great Companies Do Best" by Jim Collins and Jerry Porras, analyzed many strong companies which had managed to achieve greatness with a firmly-held set of core values that did not change, although operations, products and many other things did change. Core values, which might include things like integrity, quality, service, innovation, or human relationships, should be expressed in the authentic language of the organization's people. And to really make them stick, again leaders must "walk the talk," demonstrating to everyone that they take these values seriously and use them as guides for making decisions.

Like the vision statement, core values are best developed by a small leadership group in draft form, then circulated to all personnel for feedback and refinement. Even more than a vision statement, people will hold you accountable for core values. The more effort that goes into developing them, the more people expect they will actually be used to make critical decisions. If you say, "People are our most important asset," then lay off a lot of them during a recession or merger, it will undermine the whole value set and their strength as guides for enduring success.

Creating a Challenging Mission

3. Create a challenging mission. Many organizations consider vision and mission interchangeable. We prefer the distinction that a vision states "what we want to become" and a mission states "what we must do to achieve the vision." With a little thought, certain logically necessary courses of action follow from the commitment to a defining vision. For example, if you want to be the leading health-care architect in the Southeast specializing in wellness centers, your mission might consist of things like:

- Continuously educating our people on innovations and best practices in wellness centers worldwide.
- Attracting, retaining and developing architects who are committed to wellness center design and highly talented at doing that.

- Monitoring competitors in the Southeast, including out-of-region firms seeking to do business here, so that we know what type of work they are doing and can make sure we stay ahead.
- Attending or presenting seminars on wellness, the principles behind it, and how that translates into good facility design.
- Seeking news media coverage highlighting our expertise in wellness centers, and engaging in other promotions such as direct mail to potential clients and a dynamic website.

Again it is desirable to get a high degree of participation from throughout the organization in developing the mission statements, but the list should be short, typically between 4 and 8 action item, and highly specific to your organization, not a generic list.

Setting a Few Key Goals

4. Set a few key goals. We like the SMART goal concept: a goal should be Specific, Measurable, Achievable, Realistic and Timed. Many people set goals such as "increase our revenues" or "hire more people" that are in the right direction but are not really SMART. Some people call these vague goals "fuzzies." An example of a SMART goal (depending on the organization) would be: "Increase revenues by 10% in the next 12 months." Or "Hire at least two new professionals within six months."

Too many goals can lead to analysis paralysis. This is actually fairly common when organizations try to do their own strategic planning. To make sure there is something for everybody, well-intending organizations create pages and pages of goals which are really no more than wish lists, because they cannot all be achieved. In today's intense, busy, fast-changing workplace, it is far better to have a *few key goals* to help people focus their improvement efforts. By contrast, the more those efforts are spread thin, the less progress you'll see a year from now. Even some large organizations have only about three key goals a year so they can really focus on making them happen. That is so important. They must be challenging, but if they are not achieved, it will be an emotional downer for the whole company, and hard to get people excited about other goals anytime soon.

Goals should challenge people to stretch, to do their best, but not create unbearable pressure and add to their stress. A balance between easy and impossible must be carefully struck by the goal-setting process.

Developing a Strategy for Each Goal

5. Develop a strategy for each goal. Just as the mission explains how the organization will achieve the vision, strategies explain how the organization will achieve the goals. (I am speaking here in traditional strategic planning terms – we will discuss the new living-systems view of strategy shortly.) The rhythm of "pick a target, figure how to get there" can resonate all the way through objectives and tactics, but increasingly companies are leaving those details to departments and not trying to set them in stone at the corporate level.

One of the main reasons many organizations' plans fail is because the goals are not backed by realistic how-to strategies. Current thinking is for upper management to propose the top key goals, pass them to the responsible people for feedback and to make sure they will be supported, then let those responsible for implementation work out the strategies, again passing them back up the line to make sure executives approve. Strategies should include five key elements:

- **Actions** to be taken, stated in broad terms but adequately specific to give direction.
- **Responsibilities** for those actions, with responsible people fully committing to the actions.
- **Timing** - when they will occur.
- **Budget** - where the money is coming from, and how much.
- **Metrics** - how progress toward each goal will be measured and communicated.

Another check to be sure you've got a full strategy is to ask the old journalism questions, Who, What, When, Where, Why, How and (one I always add) How Much.

The best strategies are worked out in authentic brainstorming sessions. Participants create alternative solutions in a free-wheeling, no-criticism, creative process. (It is forbidden to judge or criticize someone else's ideas in the creative session.) Then they step back and choose the most promising strategy, or combine several elements into a new one.

Once these key strategic planning steps have been taken, the challenge is to actually implement the plan day to day, and keep it up to date. Some highly disciplined organizations methodically update their strategic plans annually, insist that all budgeted programs are consistent with the strategic plan, and do a major revision every five years or sooner as needs dictate.

In the late 20th and early 21st Centuries, more attention has been directed at *implementation and execution* than at strategic planning *per se*. One major reason for this is the rapid pace of change which makes any long-range planning increasingly difficult. Another reason is that a lot of people had the experience of participating in developing a strategic plan which was never implemented. It became the proverbial notebook gathering dust on a shelf. The new action-oriented approach is also more consistent with the living-systems model we've mentioned earlier. Now let's look at different aspects of the living-systems perspective on strategy and implementation, which you may like better than traditional strategic planning, depending on your personality type.

The Living Systems Perspective

A major reason most strategic plans fail is because they are thick documents that (a) people can't keep in their heads and (b) can only be changed once a year or longer — when in reality some kind of change happens weekly if not daily to many organizations.

In the 21st Century organizations are increasingly measuring their progress toward a few key goals all the time. A number of businesses and organizations have adopted *The Balanced Scorecard* (see the book by that name for details). It emphasizes measuring four key areas of progress: Learning & Growth (human resource development, employee satisfaction, information systems etc.), Internal Business Processes (quality control, cycle time etc.), Customers (satisfaction, market share etc.) and Financial (income, profits etc.).

One point well made by *The Balanced Scorecard* is: If you are only measuring financial results, you are using *past-performance* data and "driving by looking in the rear-view mirror." Financial results are *lagging indicators* of progress. By contrast, Learning & Growth, Internal Business Processes and

Customer Relations are *leading indicators* – they come *before* the profits are earned (or not).

Some suggest that you need an "instrument panel" or "dashboard" of key measurements that are constantly updated to let you know how you are doing. This system is by definition objective, and it should be open to all key personnel. Even if you don't want to share all financial details, you can share a few key numbers like sales and profits for the month. Even more important is to measure other dimensions of performance that better enable you to predict the future rather than reflect the past. This is an important "missing element" of most strategic plans and one reason they do not work.

The newest approaches to these challenges shift the emphasis (also known as the mechanical perspective) from an "instrument panel" which suggests machines measuring objects, to information and feedback, which are vital processes for all living systems. You as a living system yourself could not get along in the world without your senses giving you a constant flow of information and feedback from the environment in which you are living and moving. As we walk, for example, millions of signals are flowing from our eyes, our feet, our ears, and other bodily parts, helping us keep our balance, move in the desired direction, and avoid obstacles.

In an organization like a business, we are all operating as individuals with all senses working, but one important thing is missing that keeps our group from functioning as a living system. Can you think of what that is?

What is missing is a continuous flow of information and feedback among the parts (people) in our system! Yes we have email, meetings, conversations and other forms of communication. But one of the main reasons human organizations fail to achieve significant and enduring success is that "the left hand doesn't know what the right hand is doing."

The Importance of Abundant Communication

Over the years my company has done many surveys and focus groups of employees of different organizations. In almost every case, the rank and file people complain of poor communication. Leaders don't let them know what is going on. They work with painfully limited information. The organization is not functioning as a true living system – it is just functioning as a collection of people under one roof.

This takes us back to the great importance of strategy as shared purpose, focus, vision and values. The more such key directional elements are truly shared, the more the organization CAN act as one united system. Not only is information shared about what is going on daily and hourly, but also information is shared about what is going on monthly, annually and long-term. The organization knows what it is and where it is going. When this sense of purpose and vision are really "alive" within each member of the organization, its success is not so dependent on the leaders at the top. It's more like a starfish that can regenerate a limb if one is cut off. The organization is a true whole, and the whole is greater than the sum of the parts. The whole has a life of its own.

Systems Thinking for Best Results

Truly effective strategy in the 21st Century requires an appreciation of the living system perspective which we portrayed as a five-factor star model earlier. The organization is understood and managed as a dynamic, interconnected system, with interdependent parts acting as a whole. Peter Senge influenced thousands of people with his 1994 best-seller, *The Fifth Discipline*, which strongly advocated *systems thinking*. (Systems thinking *is* the "fifth" discipline.) In more recent years, more and more people and organizations have adopted the *living systems* perspective. The key difference is that earlier systems thinking was based on *mechanical paradigms* such as cause and effect, also called *linear thinking*, which tends to view the organization as a machine. The newer living systems view instead emphasizes that causes and effects are interactive and interdependent. For example, in human relationships it is often impossible to say "who struck first" but more helpful to look at the interaction. I relate to you in ways influenced by how you relate to me, which is influenced by how I related to you earlier, which was influenced by how you related to me earlier, and so on back to the very start of each relationship.

Another aspect of the living systems perspective is to view an organization as a living organism, struggling to survive in a sometimes-hostile environment. Some have used the analogy of an amoeba, which changes shape as needed to absorb food or avoid danger. But a true living system in the new view is composed of multiple individuals interacting in complex ways. The important point of this living systems view is that organizations consisting of multiple people are inherently complex, involving so many interactions and interdependencies that any attempt to restrict them with a "linear" process such as traditional strategic planning is bound to have shortcomings.

The Significance of Learning

Living systems are able to adapt to the changing environment only because they have the capacity to LEARN. This is why Peter Senge and others advocated the "Learning Organization." If your organization cannot LEARN from experience in the real world, it will repeat the same mistakes over and over, and is not likely to survive very long. Since people come and go in organizations, taking the learning out of people's heads and turning it into structures and processes is vitally important and valuable. This has given rise to the relatively new field of Knowledge Management. It seeks to capture the knowledge of the people in the organization and use it as a database to guide smarter decisions in the future. But this requires the resources of a fairly large organization and is not something most small businesses can sustain.

Adapting to the Changing Environment

However, at the very least, successfully adapting to the changing environment does require *observing* the environment and talking about it within the management team. This in turn requires reading newspapers, magazines and electronic media, going to professional association meetings and trade shows, keeping a finger on the pulse of the marketplace and the competition. Often this happens informally, as one person will tell another something he observed or learned about. But if it is formalized in the sense of being regularly discussed at management meetings, put in writing, and shared internally, the power of continuous adaptation can be made much more effective.

Human communication is so difficult, the only way to avoid costly mistakes is to *over-communicate*, especially on critical projects or processes. A central shared database, password-protected, is one way to do that. But most small organizations don't have the manpower to sustain that. Instead, all of us can keep in mind this important truth: the greater the possibility of *misunderstanding*, the more important *face-to-face* communication becomes. Some experts claim that 80 percent of effective interpersonal communication is nonverbal! Often body language, facial expression, tone of voice and other nonverbal cues communicate more than just words on paper or email.

Interrelationships with Other Success Factors

Finally, as a checklist for ensuring effective 21st-Century strategy, consider its interrelationships with the other Key Success Factors with questions like these:

- Has our strategy been created with the full involvement of our **people**, and does it reflect what they care about and are committed to?
- Has our strategy been created with the full involvement of our **markets**, with objective research or surveys into the needs, perceptions and preferences of customers, prospects, and others outside of the organization?
- Have we thought through the **operational** aspects of implementing our strategy on a day to day basis, so it becomes a part of our on-going work and internal processes?
- Have we considered the **financial** aspects of our strategy, how we are going to pay for these initiatives, and how we are going to ensure the continuing financial strength of the organization? Does our strategy include considerations for our facilities, equipment, and pay structure?

So, to summarize, the Strategy Success Factor has several key components which, united into a system, keep the organization on track, keep everyone singing off the same page, keep customers happy, keep competitors in the dust, keep the money rolling in, keep the profits up. That's why I consider Strategy the No. 1 Essential Success Factor.

References:

The Balanced Scorecard: Translating Strategy Into Action, by Robert Kaplan and David Norton:
http://www.amazon.com/exec/obidos/ASIN/0875846513/wwwlciwebcom

A POWERFUL SYSTEM FOR TOTAL BUSINESS SUCCESS

The Fifth Discipline: The Art and Practice of the Learning Organization, by Peter Senge:
http://www.amazon.com/exec/obidos/ASIN/0385260954/wwwlciwebcom

Built To Last: Successful Habits of Visionary Companies, by Jim Collins and Jerry Porras
http://www.amazon.com/exec/obidos/ASIN/0060516402/wwwlciwebcom

Key Success Factor No. 2: People

Part 1: Lessons Learned from Experience

"People" are the key to business success, as all us people know. But "people" as a success factor is like the weather – everybody talks about it, but often no one does anything about it. Part 2 of this chapter reports on the very impressive people-management principles of *First, Break All The Rules*, based on extensive research. Here in Part 1, we will share with you some practical insights we've gained from personal experience and other information sources.

Once I saw an interview of legendary GE Chairman Jack Welch, one of the most admired manager-leaders of modern times, on the Charlie Rose Show. It was interesting that, while GE famously aspired to be No.1 or No. 2 in every market it competes in, Welch claimed that their core competence is *developing people*. GE and a few other big companies have cultures that strongly encourage effective management and people development, but in the vast majority of companies, that does not happen. Here are a few key truths about people as a success factor which may be helpful for you:

1. That which gets reinforced gets repeated. Michael LeBoeuf a few years ago wrote a great little book called, *The Greatest Management Principle in the World*, and this greatest principle is, "That which gets reinforced gets repeated." This powerful reinforcement principle of psychology and human behavior was discovered by B.F. Skinner and has been rejected by some people because it applies as much to rats in a cage as it does to humans. And guess what? It works just as well on both (including kids). If you want somebody to repeat a behavior, reinforce it with some type of reward that they will appreciate. That might be as simple as saying "Well done." If you want somebody to stop a behavior, withdraw the reinforcement. And interestingly, the most powerful way to *sustain* a behavior is through *intermittent* reinforcement. If a child (or employee) wants something that is not in the firm's best interests, and you give in just a couple of times, that habit will be more deeply ingrained than if you gave in every time, then suddenly stopped. Consistency is extremely important in shaping people's behavior.

2. Different strokes for different folks. Because people are fundamentally unique individuals, what one considers a reward, another may consider punishment. The most widely used personality profiling system in the world, the Myers-Briggs Type Indicator, features 16 different personality types, each with its own preferred strokes. If you know your people's types, you can give them the strokes they want; if not, you run the risk of giving them strokes *against* their grain by treating them the way *you* want to be treated, not the way *they* want to be treated.

3. You cannot not communicate. That axiom, from the classic little book *The Pragmatics of Human Communication*, refers to the fact that *not communicating* with someone says to them, "I don't care about you." When my firm does studies of nonmanagerial employees, we *always* find that they consider internal communication to be inadequate. Managers get busy putting out fires and trying to be sure customers' needs are met, and they forget the importance of communicating with everyone about what's going on with the company. They may rationalize that by thinking, "I'm in charge and I know what I'm doing," but all the employees see is the stone wall of silence.

People want to know what is going on and how it does or will affect them, and you cannot overdo that or fake it. Open communication shows people you care about them. *Not* communicating says you *don't* care about them, even if you really do. The most effective communication is always face to face. Face time says "I care about you" like nothing else. Even if you do not agree, even if you cannot give the person what they want, genuine listening is very valuable in communicating caring. Avoid emails or memos for any information which might be misunderstood or possibly construed as negative.

4. You can't change people; change the system. By the time someone is 21 or 22, their personalities and behaviors are so set that nothing is going to change *them* except a significant emotional event. Such an event might be marriage, divorce, the birth of a child, the death of a loved one, or getting fired from a long-held job. It is hard to engineer positive emotional events at work that are significant and appropriate. Some teams go whitewater rafting or wilderness hiking to share emotional experiences. But generally speaking, you cannot change people, so instead you change the system of rewards that reinforce desired behaviors, or in rare cases, punish unacceptable behaviors (generally punishment backfires and creates deep resentment, even rebellion).

For example, if quality is important, you create a *system* that measures and rewards high quality. You don't preach to your people or put up signs that say, "Remember, don't make mistakes!" And you walk the talk by demonstrating your own passion for quality - or whatever behavioral change you are trying to instill.

5. If you want something changed, ask the doers first. Before initiating change or "improvements," let the people who will be responsible for implementation have a say in the way the changes will be handled. That is obvious but so often not done. Even if you go against their preferences, people appreciate being heard, respect you for asking, and will be more likely to follow whatever the outcome. If you do not ask, it is amazing how people can resist in many subtle ways that ultimately sabotage the outcome.

6. When you ask for people's input, respond quickly. We've been involved in a number of situations where employees' hopes were raised through focus groups or other input, but in spite of our recommendations, management did not act on what people said. Again you do not have to do what your people suggest. But employee emotions are extremely time sensitive. You lift their hopes when you seek their input, and if you act on that input, you sustain their enthusiasm and energies. If you wait too long, the emotional peak passes and you will not have another chance like that for a long time.

This is one reason GE has been so successful with their "workout" sessions. Everyone involved gets in one room and one manager is in charge. Discussion focuses on one problem. No one leaves the room until the top manager decides what action will be taken on the problem. The decision may be to act now or to delegate the problem to a task force if more information is essential, but some action is always taken. This is one way GE keeps their people "generally electrified" and loyal.

7. It's all about human energy. Human energy is the ultimate resource for any business. People are not just bodies but *energy systems* with mental, physical, emotional and spiritual energies, all of which can be engaged or ignored. Any planning effort or change effort will succeed best if you channel people's natural energies in the direction of the new activities. (Refer to 1 and 2 above.) Find out how each person naturally uses his or her energies through instruments like Myers-Briggs or Keirsey indicators. Try to give them roles in the new activities that let them use their natural energies effectively.

Communicate with them often – up-front and on-going. It is amazing what people will do when you work with their natural energies and encourage them along the way.

Before we move on to Part 2 of the People section, here are references for key books we've already discussed:

The Greatest Management Principle in the World (has new title) by Michael LeBoeuf, Ph. D.:
http://www.amazon.com/exec/obidos/ASIN/0425113973/wwwlciwebcom

The Pragmatics of Human Communication by Paul Watzlawick et al.:
http://www.amazon.com/exec/obidos/ASIN/0393010090/wwwlciwebcom

Please Understand Me: Character and Temperament Types, by David Keirsey, Marilyn Bates
http://www.amazon.com/exec/obidos/ASIN/0960695400/wwwlciwebcom

People, Part 2: What The World's Greatest Managers Do Differently

What do the world's greatest managers do differently? That question was asked by the Gallup Organization through in-depth interviews of over 80,000 managers in over 400 companies. This is the largest study of its kind ever undertaken, and the result was one of the top-selling books of recent years: *First, Break All The Rules: What the World's Greatest Managers Do Differently* by Marcus Buckingham & Curt Coffman. The authors identified 12 questions which absolutely nail the practices of best managers. See if you think people working for you would answer "yes" to them:

"1. Do I know what is expected of me at work?"
"2. Do I have the materials and equipment I need to do my work right?"
"3. At work, do I have the opportunity to do what I do best every day?"
"4. In the last seven days, have I received recognition or praise for good work?"
"5. Does my supervisor, or someone at work, seem to care about me as a person?"
"6. Is there someone at work who encourages my development?"
"7. At work, do my opinions seem to count?"
"8. Does the mission/purpose of my company make me feel like my work is important?"
"9. Are my co-workers committed to doing quality work?"
"10. Do I have a best friend at work?"
"11. In the last six months, have I talked with someone about my progress?"
"12. At work, have I had opportunities to learn and grow?"

The authors of "First Break" note that these questions emerged from exhaustive statistical analyses and do not represent *all* that workers want. Surveys my firm has done asking personnel "what is most important or valuable to you in your job" invariably come up with answers relating to pay, benefits, good internal communication, getting along with fellow employees and other topics. But because people at virtually all companies want these things, questions on these matters do not separate well-managed companies from poorly managed companies. So if you were to ask your people, "Is it important for you to have good pay and benefits?" practically all except the independently wealthy would answer "yes."

A POWERFUL SYSTEM FOR TOTAL BUSINESS SUCCESS

The 12 questions above are what researchers call *discriminating* questions - they discriminate well-managed organizations from those which are not. They also point out what is very important for all managers and leaders to practice to get the best performance and to retain good employees. We encourage you to read the list again and think about what would be required for your people to answer "yes" to all of them.

The management approach prevalent in many organizations today is what I call the "military/parent model." That is, management's task is seen as controlling or directing employees, keeping them out of trouble, and trying to care for them in a manner that is somewhat paternalistic or maternal. Most of us have the best intentions, it's just that this is all we know, from being parents or observing other managers, or in increasingly rare cases, serving in the armed forces. *First, Break All The Rules* shows a better way!

First, Break All The Rules: What the World's Greatest Managers Do Differently
http://www.amazon.com/exec/obidos/ASIN/0684852861/wwwlciwebcom

Part 3: A Living Systems Approach to People as a Key Success Factor

Let's take a look now at the living-system connections between People and other success factors:

- Have our people been involved in developing our strategy, and does it reflect what is important to them?
- Are our people involved in continuously improving our operations, and are our operations people-friendly, or are they "mechanical," requiring people to work like machines?
- Do our people understand what our markets – customers and prospects – want and need, how they perceive us, and how our people's behaviors profoundly influence the market's perceptions of our business or organization?
- Do our people understand how their behaviors impact company income and profits, and are they rewarded for helping to increase profits or generate new income streams?
- Are our policies and procedures people-friendly in terms of respecting obligations to family members, including children? Do we acknowledge that our people are parts not only of our company's living system, but also of other living systems, especially families and communities?

Fundamentally everyone wants to feel that the leaders of their organizations care about them as individuals with unique talents and needs. The Golden Rule has been supplanted by the Platinum Rule: *Do unto others as they want to be done unto.* Increasingly organizations are like substitute families for their people, who spend most of their waking hours at work interacting with each other. Showing people that you care about them can go a long way to boosting productivity, profits and other solid bottom-line benefits.

Now, let's look at Success Factor No. 3: Marketing.

Key Success Factor No. 3: Marketing

The first job for any business, as the great management expert Peter Drucker once noted, is getting and keeping customers. Whether you call this marketing, selling, customer relations or external communications, this, as I like to say, is *where the money comes from*. This is also the area where I have had the most personal experience, and I could write a book on this subject alone if space allowed. But instead I'm going to focus on the really, really important components we should all keep in mind and practice if we want to be successful. As with the section on Strategy, I will first give some more traditional approaches to marketing, then discuss some of the newer and more exciting innovations in the field.

Marketing for the Small Business

As a small business owner or manager, you don't have a multi-million-dollar budget for ads during half-time of the Super Bowl or for direct mail to households across the country. Your marketing budget is limited, and you want to – need to – get the biggest bang for your buck.

There are plenty of websites and books which will give you thousands of small business marketing ideas and possibilities, but there are so many choices, it can be confusing to decide: Which approach is best for you? This chapter is designed to answer that question as concisely as possible.

First of all, we need to define what we are talking about.

Small business - The Small Business Act states that a small business concern is "one that is independently owned and operated and which is not dominant in its field of operation." The federal government assumes, as a general rule, that a small business has fewer than 500 employees. In actual practice, it's fairly common to describe a small business as having fewer than 100 employees. Of course, the smaller you go, the more businesses there are, with hundreds of thousands having 10 or fewer people.

THE 5 KEY SUCCESS FACTORS

Marketing – The American Marketing Association states: "Marketing is an organizational function and a set of processes for creating, communicating and delivering value to customers and for managing customer relationships in ways that benefit the organization and its stakeholders." Got that? What this means is, importantly, marketing is not just something that a marketing person does. Marketing is a function of the whole organization, or as we like to say in this book, a part of a living system.

First of all, you create value for customers in the form of products or services they want. Second, you communicate to these existing or potential customers that you have what they want. Third, you deliver the products or services to the paying customers. And long-term you manage relationships with customers in ways that benefit your organization and its stakeholders.

We also like the simple definition: "Marketing involves orienting the business to meet the needs of the customer." Again that stresses that it is an organizational function, with meeting the needs of the customer as its main focus. Now, how do we go about doing that?

The first constraint is, you've probably already decided what your business is. And your business is probably either what you like to do, what you want to do, or what your business is already doing. The problem with this is, maybe this is not what customers want to pay money for. The No. 1 reason that so many small businesses fail, especially the newer ones, is that they do not offer products or services that enough people want to pay for!

Any town or city in America has seen restaurants, antique shops, clothing stores, consignment shops and many other retail establishments open their doors with high hopes, and close them before much time has passed, with huge debts and disappointments. It's a real heartache. The American dream becomes a nightmare. How can you keep that from happening to you? Instead of focusing mainly on what *you* want to do or what *you* like, focus on what *customers* need – and some of those needs are constantly changing, especially in the fast-paced 21st Century.

1. **Find out what customers want** – This is very important, and the step that most entrepreneurs or small business owners neglect. It is all too natural to assume that if you like something, other people will like it too, but that may

not be the case – or even if they do, they might be satisfied with their current provider. If you already have your business in operation, ask your current customers what is *most important to them* in choosing a supplier of (what you do), what you can do to increase their satisfaction, and other natural questions related to choosing a product or service provider.

If you haven't started your new business yet, ask friends and relatives what they want or like in the business field you are interested in, or how they would go about finding a company that provides it. Encourage objective answers because it won't really help you if they tell you what they think you want to hear.

If you can afford it, hire a professional market research firm. Some will do a survey for $2,000 or less. Or if you're really lucky, and a nearby college or university teaches marketing, you might be able to get a class or group of students to do your research survey for little or no money as a real-world learning exercise. It's worth a try!

2. **Analyze the competition** – If your business operates locally, just look in the Yellow Pages or do a search online and see how many companies are already in that field in your market area. The more there are, the harder it's going to be to compete effectively – not that this should necessarily stop you, but it's an indication of how hard you're going to have to work to get established. If possible, "shop" the competition by calling to ask them about their products or services, how long they have been in business, etc. As long as you don't lie, there's nothing unethical about asking questions – until you reach a point that the person answering the phone stops talking to you anyway!

Most businesses today have websites, so you can enter the name of the business into a search engine like Google or Yahoo and learn even more. Here's a tip: start by putting the business's exact name in quotes, or include the city and state, making it much more likely that the search engine will pull up that exact business you are analyzing. Of course if you are starting a business which you want to market nationally or via the Internet, it's even more valuable to use a search engine and spend time studying the websites of actual or potential competitors. As you look at them, think about how you would feel as a customer experiencing this site, and what you would communicate or do instead with your own website.

3. **Select a niche you can dominate** – Again, this is a point little understood and rarely practiced by small businesses. You cannot be all things to all people. The natural tendency when a business is young is to do anything that customers will pay you money for, and certainly cash flow is essential. But the more focused you are on a niche you can dominate, the more likely you will be able to achieve that dominant position in a relatively short amount of time (it may take a few years but not a lifetime).

    The literal meaning of "niche" is "nest," but historically it meant a small space or hollow in a wall for a religious statue or other valued object. The idea is, don't try to be the wall, and don't try to be the big stones or blocks in the wall – just carve out a little space between the big companies that's custom-shaped for you and your small business.

    Instead of being a generalist, be a specialist. Instead of selling any kind of antiques, focus on early American or Chinese antiques. Instead of doing any kind of landscaping, focus on shrubbery or roses. Instead of selling any kind of book, focus on children's books or mysteries. Instead of being a general-purpose real estate agent, focus on serving young adults or seniors. Here is the key: the niche you choose must be small enough that no one else is dominating it now, or that you could reasonably dominate in a reasonable amount of time, BUT big enough that there is sufficient demand for it.

    It's also important to select a niche with growth potential. For example, you know that the number of retired people in America and even your community is certainly going to increase as Baby Boomers reach age 65. But do not choose a niche like making shirts where foreign competition has already wiped out many American manufacturers – unless perhaps you are going to make very custom-tailored shirts for the wealthy.

    So give a lot of thought and do some research about where your target market is going in terms of trends – growing or shrinking, and why. Understand the underlying dynamics behind the trends. Pick a rising wave, not a falling tide.

    Defining your niche, then, is a combination of choosing a particular market segment and deciding what unusual products or services you will offer to that market segment that (a) build on what you know or like to do, (b) are things customers want, and (c) are not things that competitors are currently providing adequately.

4. **Planning your marketing mix** – For many years the marketing "mix" has been defined as a combination of the "4 P's" of marketing. These are the four primary variables of your marketing strategy and implementation:

(a) <u>Product</u> – the products or services you will offer to customers for sale. As noted above, you must select products or services that fill a real need, in a niche small enough that you can dominate it. But beyond just selecting your product or service, other important success factors must be carefully managed. Probably most important is quality. You need to offer products of high quality that the customer can depend on time and time again. The quality must be consistent and must conform to the customer's perceptions, not just yours. If you are in a service business – and even the act of selling products is a service – you must ensure that the whole customer experience is enjoyable. From the first point of contact with your business, through service delivery and the purchasing experience, and on to service or follow-up after the sale, every step needs to be carefully planned and managed (especially if you have employees) so the customer experiences pleasure and satisfaction at every step. Again regular honest feedback from your customers is vital to keep this customer experience not only positive but also continuously improving.

(b) <u>Price</u> – the price you will charge for your products or services. The customer not only pays money for your stuff – he or she also pays in time and effort. And the customer will consider all that when deciding to buy again. How much time or effort did the customer expend to obtain your offering? What can you do to minimize the time and effort so the purchase is exceptionally convenient and positive? Again think about the total experience and what you can do to continuously improve.

(c) <u>Place</u> – your place of business or how you deliver your products. Customers judge your business by your place of business or product distribution point even before they receive and use the product or service. Every little thing influences customer perceptions. In retail, not only is convenient location important, but also visibility from a main road, easy

THE 5 KEY SUCCESS FACTORS

access in and out, and safety all important factors in the consumers mind (sometimes unconsciously) as he or she buys from you or considers buying. The way your employees are dressed, the interior furnishings and lighting, air conditioning, smell – all the senses are working to develop a perception of your business, product and service. Attention to detail is vital.

(d) <u>Promotion</u> – communications with potential and existing customers. This is the part of marketing that most people think IS marketing, but now you see it is only a fraction of it. "If you build it, they will come" might work for a "Field of Dreams," but it doesn't work for a business of reality in most cases. It is possible for a new store or restaurant in a well-located and high-traffic shopping center to attract customers with just some nice signage and an appealing storefront. But even this kind of business, like all others, can benefit from some well-planned, creative, and well-executed promotion. Since this is so important (and what most people think marketing is), we'll devote the next whole section to it.

5. **Promoting your business** – there are over 50 different ways to promote your business through marketing communications, but generally they fall into a few major categories:

(a) <u>Advertising</u> is communication where you pay the media for carrying your message. Newspaper, radio and TV advertising can work well for businesses which sell to individuals and the public but it can be fairly expensive. The famous New York merchant John Wannamaker is reported to have said, "50 percent of my advertising is a waste. I just don't know which 50 percent." Lots of small businesses that try various forms of advertising find that much of it seems to be a waste because there are no apparent sales resulting. One way to alleviate that common problem is to use some form of response tracking. You can make specific offers in different ads, and ask customers to use the offer number when responding in order to get that particular deal. If you give coupons, of course, customers will need to bring them in to redeem them. With internet advertising a number of software programs allow you to track responses to your online ads and offers with great precision. Any way you cut it, advertising is expensive. You pay for media time and space. That's why I recommend that my customers take maximum advantage of "free" media time and space using:

(b) <u>Public Relations</u>, also called PR or publicity. The catch here is that the news media will not run the same story over and over again, as is the case with paid advertising. Instead, you must present something new – as the saying goes, "Three-fourths of NEWS is NEW." But even with a small business, there are often opportunities to get articles printed in local and sometimes national media about new products or services, new personnel or promotions, special events like seminars or open houses, and many other activities that skilled PR practitioners are good at. Companies like mine that also offer public relations services have access to huge directories of practically all news media in the U.S. and abroad. These directories tell what each magazine or newspaper is interested in, its circulation, editors, contacts and much more. Often it is easier to get articles published in national trade magazines than local newspapers, depending on your industry and city. One study found that public relations had seven times the credibility of advertising. Readers consider articles published by reputable media to be "facts," whereas advertising claims are always viewed with some skepticism.

(c) <u>Personal Selling</u> – Again this is often considered to be the "same as" marketing, especially when practiced by full-time sales professionals. But there is a big difference. Marketing involves finding out what your customers want and giving it to them. Selling is deciding what you want to produce and trying to persuade customers to buy it. In the best organizations marketing helps create demand for needed products, making the sales job much easier and more user-friendly. Personal selling is an art and a science. One book I highly recommend is called *SPIN Selling* by Neil Rackham (link below). SPIN stands for Situation, Problem, Implication, Need, a four-step process uncovered by a team of experts observing expert sales people at work. Fundamentally, the more you sincerely try to understand a potential customer's situation, and develop an offering customer-tailored to his or her needs, the more likely you are to be successful. This consultative approach is also reflected in several other popular books on selling. And this is a very different approach from having a "script" where you talk and talk and talk at the potential customer until you wear down resistance and "close."

(d) <u>Internet Marketing</u> – Marketing via the Internet is a cross between public relations and advertising. You are paying for the media - your website - and you may pay for the content as well, by hiring a web design firm. But overall the cost is much lower than print or broadcast advertising, and you can have thousands and thousands of words, depending on the richness of your site, with no extra cost. There is not sufficient space within this overall approach to the 5 success factors to go into all the intricacies of internet marketing success, which is a particular passion of mine. But fundamentally a website is just some code on a computer in cyberspace – the trick is, getting potential customers to come to your site – generating traffic as it is called. Having lots of solid content is a great way to make your site appealing to the search engines like Google, Yahoo and MSNsearch. Keeping it constantly updated and refreshed enhances its appeal to search engines. But with all the hundreds of millions of websites online, with millions more being added all the time, getting free traffic requires what is called Search Engine Optimization (SEO). This means optimizing individual pages for certain keywords which potential customers are likely to enter into search engines. Of course you have to also file your website with search engines. Just enter the keywords "internet marketing" into a major search engine and you will find tons of information, some valuable and much of it designed to sell you an online e-book or series of CDs. Or contact me and I will be glad to help you attract more traffic to your website.

Other Approaches to Marketing

1. Managing Customer Value. If you haven't read the marvelous book by that name (see link below) by Bradley Gale, I highly recommend it. It has had a huge impact on the marketing profession and my practice. "Customer value" is the whole package of what customers want from you -- generally some combination of quality, price and service, but always uniquely expressed by each customer or market segment.

We have conducted many customer surveys for our clients, exploring customer value, and we have always found this process to be very illuminating. After asking customers what they value most in a supplier of X (the product or services of our client), we then ask them to rate the importance of each factor.

Then we ask them to rate their satisfaction with how well our client provides each value component. The result is a neat bar chart which shows the relative importance of each factor, overlayed by a line graph which represents that company's average "score."

For one manufacturer, we discovered that, while customers were quite satisfied with quality and service, there was a big dissatisfaction gap in price. This was something our client was vaguely aware of, but when they saw the chart, they were motivated to act. They rolled out a lower-cost product in time for the next national trade show, and it was a huge success.

There's much more to Managing Customer Value than this, but the point is: "value" used to be a vague concept, but thanks to Bradley Gale, it is now measurable in several ways, a "metric" every bit as solid and useful as sales and expense numbers. And just like financials, customer value and satisfaction should be measured and charted continuously.

2. Continuous Customer Communications. Customers' needs change from time to time, and you need a way to hear that clearly. In my experience most small businesses NEVER ask their customers, "How are we doing? What can we do to improve your satisfaction?" The reason for that, I think, is business leaders don't really want to know. If sales are up, they don't think they need to know. If sales are down, they don't want to hear bad news.

It does indeed take courage to ask customers about their satisfaction. But another obstacle is that customers will rarely tell their provider what they really think. If you survey your own customers, they are likely to tell you ***what they think you want to hear***, not the real truth. The way around that is to use an objective professional research firm, and it can be much less expensive than you think.

Recently we were doing a survey for a professional service client, and one of their customers was intrigued by our questions, including customer value and satisfaction. He told our interviewer, "You know, I realized in answering these questions that I would not say the same thing to my contact in that company. I can see there is real value in having an outside firm do this. Tell me how you come up with the questions, and what you do with the answers." And so we did.

For large financial or retail firms, where customer contact is frequent and the exchange relatively impersonal (buying a product, making a deposit etc.), Richard Whitely, author of **Customer-Centered Growth** (see below) recommends what he calls "hardwiring the voice of the customer." This means that every single person who has customer contact is encouraged to capture comments, good or bad, and feed them into their central database. Some companies condense that information every day and feed it to key staff members in a concise report. Now *that* is continuous customer communication! The point is: Ask your customers what they want, listen to what they say, and act accordingly. This is one of the most powerful keys to success, so often ignored.

3. Positioning your brand. One of the great classics of marketing, ***Positioning:The Battle for Your Mind***, by Al Ries and Jack Trout, changed the world of marketing and advertising forever. Positioning has nothing to do with physical location but with the "space between the ears" (the minds) of your customers and prospects. Ries and Trout claimed (and no one disagreed) that we all perceive things in our environment in categories, often hierarchical. For example, Pepsi and Coke continue to battle for the No. 1 position on the dark cola "ladder." Luxury cars, family cars, compact cars, SUVs and other vehicles compete in their categories for dominance.

More recently it has become fashionable to speak of "branding" instead of "positioning." But the point is the same. Your brand is perceived in relation to other alternative products or services. If you cannot be No. 1 or No. 2 in a category, as Ries and Trout point out, then reposition and create your own category. You must clearly state what is different about your brand, and it must be true.

For example, we worked with a talented architect/developer who was creating a "Traditional Neighborhood Development" with inviting porches, wide sidewalks, traditional architectural design, and shops within easy walking distance. However there are a growing number of "TND's" in the metro area, some of which "got there first." With some analysis we realized that our client's development was distinctive in that all the homes are all unique and custom-built, not "production houses" similar externally and internally. So we positioned our client's development as "The Custom-Built Traditional Neighborhood." That phrase captured a very important customer value, distinguished them from the competition, and was a true claim others could not make.

Be wary of really vague or esoteric claims like we've seen with some ads by high-tech companies. If the target market doesn't "get it" instantly, you're wasting your money. Also try to focus on a ***sustainable competitive advantage***. It needs to be something that is really core to your business, a major customer value, and not the latest bell or whistle of the moment. Otherwise once your competitor adds their bell or whistle, you lose your advantage.

4. Use multiple media. A big mistake many companies make is to rely too much on advertising, which is not only very expensive but also reaches many people who would never be interested in becoming customers. Advertising is certainly valuable for those who can afford it, but we have done many marketing surveys over the years asking people, "What is the best way to communicate with you about a new provider of (this product/service)?"

You know what the answer is, about two thirds of the time, across all business categories? "Send me some information in the mail, then call me after I've had time to read it."

If someone is important enough that you want them as a customer, personalize your communication with a brief cover letter, include a nice brochure or other sales materials, and call them, without fail, a couple of days after they've received it. So many people mail but never call, and so many call but never mail. The combination is dynamite, and one we've found to be most effective for our business (besides the best one of all, referrals). It is especially effective for services, business-to-business, or big-ticket product sales. For inexpensive consumer products, the cost per sale of mailing plus follow-up may be too high, so that's where mass-media advertising works best.

One other often overlooked form of promotion is public relations. Thousands of trade journals and periodicals out there are hungry for good articles. For less than the cost of a 1-inch ad, we've placed PR articles for clients in national trade publications, read by their target markets, running 3 or 4 pages in length with photos. Obviously the interest level and credibility of such articles is far greater than paid ads and so, so much cheaper!

And no list would be complete without the wonderful Web. In addition to content-rich websites, we highly recommend that you have an email newsletter or "ezine" that allows you to keep in touch with customers and let them know about new products and services. The wonderful thing about ezines is they are absolutely free to distribute, as opposed to the printing and mailing costs of paper newsletters.

If you market to consumers, social media such as Facebook, Twitter and YouTube can be great ways to attract new customers and retain existing ones, although this requires daily attention and time for best results.

5. **One-To-One Marketing**. This phrase, popularized by Don Peppers and Martha Rogers' great book, ***The One To One Future*** (link below), is based on an approach many of us have learned over the years. The way I like to express this great truth is, "The unit of marketing is the relationship between two individual people." What this means is, people want to be treated and known as individuals.

The best way to facilitate this is with a computer database which keeps track of each customer or prospect's contact information, characteristics and preferences. Some Customer Relationship Management (CRM) software will pull up a customer's key information file automatically when caller ID identifies their incoming phone call. If that doesn't work, their name or phone number manually entered will pull it up. But on an even more personal basis, have one person assigned as THE contact person for each customer. For large-potential sales, encourage your personnel to build personal relationships with key customers. Find out about their likes, hobbies, families and more, and capture it in a protected database. Correctly used, computers can ***increase*** customer intimacy and loyalty. But only when that company-customer contact is experienced as one to one, person to person.

6. **Caring for customers**. The importance of caring for customers is aptly captured in the expression, "I don't care how much you know until I know how much you care." We are all human beings who want to feel other people love and care for us, and tapping in to that need is one of the most powerful, if not the ultimate, customer relationship methods anyone can use. This doesn't mean erotic love for customers, of course, but it does mean that we need to convince our customers we really care about what's best for them, not just getting their money. How do we do that? A few key ways:

- Show an interest in customers as persons. Listen to them with empathy. Remember what they say. Record key information in a database so you and others don't forget.
- Give something extra. Provide a small product or service for free, as an expression of appreciation, not just at Christmas but unexpectedly, or give a special discount.
- Begin with a needs assessment. This is a powerful tool which some professionals use regularly but many other businesses can learn to do. This shows you really want to understand what your customers need and are not just trying to sell them something off the shelf or something that someone else bought. (Marketing is giving people what they want and need; selling is trying to persuade people to buy what you want to provide.)
- Remember to say "thank you." Don't take anyone's business for granted. Let them know you appreciate their business by explicitly telling them so.

In closing, I'd like to say "thank you" for reading this book and applying its teachings.

References:

- ***Managing Customer Value: Creating Quality and Service that Customers Can See:***
  http://www.amazon.com/exec/obidos/ASIN/0029110459/wwwlciwebcom
- ***Customer-Centered Growth: Five Proven Strategies for Building Competitive Advantage:***
  http://www.amazon.com/exec/obidos/ASIN/0201154935/wwwlciwebcom
- ***Positioning: The Battle For Your Mind:***
  http://www.amazon.com/exec/obidos/ASIN/0446347949/wwwlciwebcom
- ***SPIN Selling***
  http://www.amazon.com/exec/obidos/ASIN/0070511136/wwwlciwebcom

- ***The One to One Future: Building Relationships One Customer at a Time***
  http://www.amazon.com/exec/obidos/ASIN/0385485662/wwwlciwebcom

Key Success Factor No. 4: Operations
... Or, What You Do All Day

Not long ago we conducted a **Customer Value & Satisfaction Survey** for a small-business client. His customers told us that they were generally satisfied with the company's people and professionalism, but they felt improvements were needed in quality control, attention to detail and follow-through. These are common *operations* issues, though by no means the only ones, concerning what your people do all day. In this chapter I'll share with you what I told my survey client, and what I'd tell you if you want to improve your operations and success.

1. Improvements must be driven from the top. Operations improvements cannot be delegated to a committee (unless you lead it) or left to a consultant's intervention. You as the manager-leader model the corporate culture of those who report to you. So you must have a passion for operations improvement in your gut, or it will not happen.

Essentially, changing any organization requires a *new energy force* moving in a direction different from business as usual. You might conjure up that energy within you just by thinking about how messed up your operations are. Or maybe you get the results from a customer survey that show distinct dissatisfaction. All too often it takes a crisis like a big drop in income or the loss of a major client to shake an organization into a state of readiness for operations improvement.

In his excellent book *Leading Change* (link below), John Kotter advocates that you stimulate energy by creating a sense of urgency. Maybe there is indeed a crisis. Or maybe you "engineer" one to make your point. However you get the energy going, you the manager-leader have to drive it.

2. The fundamental purpose of operations is to align what people do all day with what customers value. In previous chapters we've talked about the importance of customer value. If you want to improve your operations, build a system to guarantee delivery of the value which customers want. If your customers want quality, build a system that checks quality at every key step, not just at the end. If your customers want speed, study ways to cut out time-wasting steps and replace them with consolidated simpler ones, perhaps using computer systems to make things move faster.

The key point here is, don't just look at your operations and ask yourself, "How can we improve this?" Start instead with what customers value most, step back from day-to-day habits, and try to design an ideal system for delivering that value consistently. Again you'll find some excellent tips on this in Bradley Gale's *Managing Customer Value*. I also recommend reading at least one good book on *Total Quality Management*, such as the Portable MBA Series' title by that name.

3. Involve your people in operations improvement. Don't come down from the mountain like Moses with your new Ten Commandments. Let all your people get involved in analyzing and designing how operations can be improved to deliver greater customer value. It never ceases to amaze me how "ordinary people" can come up with great insights for improving operations. After all, they're often the ones closest to the action, or the ones who hear the complaints. Involving your people will not only yield a much greater abundance of good ideas, it will also greatly strengthen the likelihood that improvements will happen.

If you have a big company and it's not practical to involve everyone in the whole change process, then organize what John Kotter calls a "guiding coalition." This is not just the top people but a cross-section involving all levels. Be politically shrewd and include people who have a lot of personal power and influence at lower levels even if they are not managers. Consider involving even your chronic rebels. They often have a lot of energy and strength, and by being involved in the improvement process, they will come to support it and advocate it with others.

4. Measure what matters. Some companies have found a comprehensive measurement system like *The Balanced Scorecard* to be a great way to measure performance of all the success factors we're writing about in this series. Others try to measure too many things and get bogged down in minutiae. I recently read about a financial company that expected managers to monitor and be judged based on over 200 measurement points! So the trick is to pick just a few key indicators of improvement, measure them continuously, and share the results.

I like the analogy of driving a car with simple measurements such as the speedometer, odometer, gas gauge, and warning lights. In fact some people use the term "dashboard" to refer to the ideal small set of measurements that help people stay on course. (Contrast that with the controls of a 747 jet, which require a crew of people to monitor and control.) For example:

- If you want to improve quality, count mistakes as well as fault-free results.
- If you want to improve speed, track cycle time, how long it takes your people to complete a defined task.
- If you want to improve customer satisfaction and retention, track complaints, or better yet do a frequent short customer survey that is meaningful enough to allow specific feedback, not just a generic restaurant-type card. Be sure to seek information on changing customer needs and preferences or this year's solution will be obsolete next year.

It is amazing how just the simple act of measuring a performance indicator and posting the results with either a wall chart or on your internal computer network can motivate people to do better, especially if there is a clear link between their own performance and one or more indicators. In fact it is very important for people to understand that linkage. Ideally individual performance is also measured and rewarded in terms consistent with your corporate measurement system.

5. Control products and services differently. If you are a manufacturer, controlling operations by measuring physical products is fairly straightforward compared with measuring services. Most books on quality, operations or business process improvement are written from the manufacturing perspective. If you're in the service business, don't think these books are going to do you much good. A few determined service businesses have indeed been successful with TQM or ISO9000, and my hat's off to them. But the amount of time wasted by service businesses (including mine) trying to adopt manufacturing-based operations methodology is staggering.

One of the best, classic books on service quality is *Delivering Service Quality* by Valarie Zeithaml et al. This research/authoring team was the first to define service quality as a matter of "balancing customer perceptions and expectations." Since then there have been a bunch of books on the subject, as you'll see if you type "service quality" into the search window at amazon.com. Service quality essentially:

THE 5 KEY SUCCESS FACTORS

- Is a matter of customer perceptions; for customers *perception is reality*.
- Can be influenced by carefully *managing customer expectations*.
- Is *individualized for every company*, based on their customer relationships, skills, history, community, competitors and many other factors. So you have to chart your own path, but ask your customers which direction to follow.

References:

- ***Managing Customer Value: Creating Quality and Service that Customers Can See:***
  http://www.amazon.com/exec/obidos/ASIN/0029110459/wwwlciwebcom
- ***Leading Change:***
  http://www.amazon.com/exec/obidos/ASIN/0201154935/wwwlciwebcom
- ***Positioning: The Battle For Your Mind:***
  http://www.amazon.com/exec/obidos/ASIN/0446347949/wwwlciwebcom
- ***The One to One Future : Building Relationships One Customer at a Time***
  http://www.amazon.com/exec/obidos/ASIN/0385485662/wwwlciwebcom

A POWERFUL SYSTEM FOR TOTAL BUSINESS SUCCESS

Key Success Factor No. 5: Finances and Facilities

Finances and Facilities are closely intertwined, since owned facilities are both financial investments and financial assets, and rented facilities are a major expense. We don't claim to be financial advisors, but we've managed our own company's finances for over 25 years and seen a lot of companies have financial problems. So here are a few timely financial success tips from one who's been on the firing line.

1. Cash flow is king. It doesn't matter much how much your company, product or service *could* make. What matters, your lifeblood, is, do you have the cash today to pay your bills? The main reason so many dot-coms became dot-bombs is they used their cash (from investors) so fast they called it (and still do) "burn rate." That's like living at home and having your parents pay all the bills -- not the real world.

To succeed in business or other endeavors, you have to watch your cash flow very carefully. Accrual accounting is great for forecasting your success, but it does not reflect cash in the bank, so you need to watch both to know where your business stands. In fact, if you are a top company officer, you should watch your cash flow so carefully that you have an intuitive feel for it. That way if something goes wrong (like embezzling or a sudden income drop) you can sense the problem and check it out.

2. Cash flow is always cyclical. I have never seen a business yet that did not have ebbs and flows in cash volume. The cycle may be annual or multi-year, but those who've been around a while learn that there's a real law of nature -- "to everything there is a season, a time to reap and a time to sow". When your cash flow is strong, it is so tempting to spend it and so wise to save some. Financial conservatism always pays big dividends.

I remember years ago talking to an old entrepreneur who had turned a small business into a major manufacturer of boots for the Army and was a multimillionaire. He seemed to be just a basic "good old boy," as they say in the South. I asked him, in effect, how did he get to be so rich? And I'll never forget his answer: "By not spending money." He manufactured Army boots in a former school building out in the country, which he no doubt acquired very cheaply.

Before you sign that lease for the expensive office or buy all that new furniture, be sure there will be a whole lot of cash in the bank left over for essentials like payroll in the inevitable slow times. That way you will be more likely to survive much longer.

3. You cannot save yourself out of a hole. I've seen many companies hit hard times and try to cut, cut, cut to get out of the hole. Cutting expenses can help, but it almost never helps as much as increasing sales. Severe cutting tends to make the patient bleed to death. Morale hits bottom and instills a negative mindset.

Instead adopt what psychologist Wayne Dyer calls "an abundance mentality." There's tons of business out there, and if you've followed our other Success Factor tips, you know how to target your markets, sharpen your advantage and go for it. Keep your spirits up and go cheerfully after new business. Price your products/services aggressively and "optionally" (our next point). Be a joy to work with. "The Lord helps those who help themselves." Self-mutilation is not the way out of the hole.

4. Offer more than one suit on the rack. That saying is from a former client who did not like me to tell him, "This one solution is just right for you." He liked choices and options. Again I've seen many companies back themselves into a hole by offering a very limited line of products or services. They get it fixed in their heads that a Model 2034X is worth $199,000, or an audit is worth $29,000 or whatever. They forget that no product or service is *intrinsically* worth anything. Things are worth exactly what people (the market) are willing to pay.

But even beyond the issue of market-demand pricing, offer your customers several options, but not so many that they are confusing or slow down the sales process. Everybody likes choices. My company rarely bids one price on any big project -- we prefer to provide at least 3 options (low, medium and high) and let the client decide. Inevitably if we forget this principle and offer a one-suit solution, the client starts backing off or resisting. Of course you have to learn -- in some cases create -- options by thinking about what you can count (if not products, count hours, visits, pages, meetings etc. and use that to quantify your options for the client).

Some professions such as architecture, building and construction unfortunately are in a difficult tradition. They almost always bid jobs in fixed numbers (dollars or percentage). In no way does this allow for problems beyond their control, for overly demanding customers or many other variables. They can also lose a bid on a slim margin. So my advice to anyone who is caught in the fixed-price trap is: offer every customer more than one suit on the rack.

Options, options, options are the way to win-win engagements that are more profitable for you and leave the customer feeling in control because he/she made the choices! You'd be amazed all the options you can "unbundle" from traditional service packages to give your clients all the options they'd ever want. Don't overdo it, of course, because too many choices can lead to analysis paralysis. Just offer options which other customers have wanted or considered or might reasonably want.

5. Know what everything really costs. Cost-accounting is not just CPA rocket science. If you treat every job as a project, and allocate time and expenses by project code, you can know fairly well whether any project made or lost money. If you don't do this, buy some project-billing or tracking software and start tracking. This is essential for any business because, if you don't know what each output product or service costs to compare with what it sells for, you can't know if you're making any profit on it.

Personally I believe every product or service should aim to make a profit. On one hand, if you're really hard up, there's the old saying, "Some money is better than no money." But if you go into a job knowing you're going to lose, or thinking you'll do a loss-leader then charge more the second time, there often is no second time, and you get burned.

Perhaps you've heard the story of the old merchant who bought T-shirts for $1.00 and sold them for 95 cents. A friend of his said, "Alvin, how do you ever expect to get rich selling shirts for less than they cost you?" Alvin quickly replied, "The volume! Think of the volume!"

Don't let it happen to you.

6. The customer never buys a product or service. The customer buys value. That is a paraphrase of Bradley Gale's great book, *Managing Customer Value*, which we've mentioned before. If you want to increase sales and profits, give the customer more value. How do you do that? You begin with a customer survey (or better yet use a professional survey firm to help). Find out exactly what the customer values when selecting a supplier like your firm. Don't guess--it's a lot more complicated than top quality at lowest price with great service. Other factors such as fast turn-around, innovation and image (Mercedes, BMW, Polo etc.) are also important in many sectors.

One of the best ways to offer more value than your competitors, to justify an equal or higher price, is to provide more information. Don't just give an ordinary product or service. Give the customer extra information about how to use what you sell to enhance their business or life. Help the customer avoid traps. Go beyond the Golden Rule to the Platinum Rule: Do unto others as *they* would have you do unto them. The added value you offer may not mean added costs for either party, but it sure can mean added customer satisfaction, retention, or that favorite '90s phrase, "customer delight."

7. You are judged by the company they see. Just a closing note about facilities as a success factor. People, especially prospective customers, gain such a strong impression of your corporate personality (e.g., trustworthiness, professionalism) when they visit your space, it is very hard to undo any negative impressions. Now if your customer never visits your hole in the wall, no problem. But rather than "our work speaks for itself," unfortunately research has shown that your place of business speaks such volumes that your prospect may never get past that powerful perception of your space.

Generally lawyers, accountants and physicians who charge big bucks all know this. And if you want to come across as the low-cost provider, you don't need or want leather chairs or oriental rugs. But that doesn't mean your customer or prospect is going to enjoy sitting in your waiting room in a chair that feels and smells like a sweaty dog or gliding across your brown linoleum floor, even if it is polished.

If you need new or improved space, I highly recommend hiring an experienced architect. The best ones are interested not only in designing your new building or expansion, but in helping you manage your facility throughout its lifecycle.

Chapter 7: Integrating the 5 Key Success Factors With A Total Success System™

The time has come to combine all **5 Key Success Factors** into an integrated system to maximize your success, what we call a **Total Success System™**. The Total Success System (TSS) is best illustrated with this diagram, which we introduced earlier in this book:

Here you see the **5 Key Success Factors** arranged in a star formation, with arrows indicating a predominant flow. The point is to demonstrate that all factors are interrelated, with connections to all the other factors at the same time. But actually it does not matter that much how we illustrate the 5 factors – which one is on top, which one comes next – since this is a simplification of complex reality, and all factors are interconnected in three dimensional space plus time. Here's how this understanding can help you:

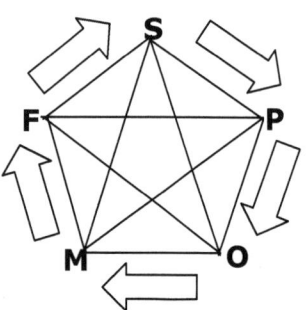

1. Your organization functions as a total system, a whole which is greater than the sum of its parts, whether you want it to or not. All the parts are connected and interdependent. If something happens to one, it affects the others, and so forth. You cannot work on one of these Success Factors effectively without acknowledging its linkages with the others. For example, Strategy should be developed with the input of your People and Markets, among other constituents.

2. For optimum success, it is essential to have these factors congruent. Most importantly your people and operations need to be congruent with what customers want and need. *Congruent* means "having mutual agreement or conformity." A popular way to say this is "in synch." Operations should be designed to produce value for customers, and people should be focused on creating that value – and continuously improving it. Strategy is the overarching big plan, but unless it is aligned with your finances, you will have problems. If you reflect on this diagram and think about the relationships between each pair of Success Factors, you begin to see how this can be a guide to action. It's simple enough to remember, but complex enough to deal with a wide variety of situations and challenges.

3. In developing your strategic or long-range plans, this Total Success System diagram can serve as **a valuable reminder to be sure you have all the key factors covered**. I once worked with a client group who had a lot of ideas which we began putting on the board. Then we sorted the ideas into the 5 Success Factors and found out that there was not one single point related to the organization's people! Some of them were participating in the meeting, but no one voiced how important it was to include people/staff development/training in the strategic plan. A corellary of this is, everything you manage or control can be put into one of these 5 Success Factor "buckets" if you understand them adequately.

4. When you go to implement a plan of any kind, you run into the problem that certain issues or responsibilities affect everybody and cannot be neatly pigeonholed into an existing <u>functional department</u> like manufacturing, sales or service. In industry it is increasingly common to deal with these problems through organizing <u>cross-functional teams</u> representing different areas of the company.

One effective way to do this is to divide your people up into five teams, one for each Success Factor. If you have enough people, consider posting a sign-up sheet in the break room or on your intranet and let people sign up for what they are interested in. If you're a nonprofit, mix up board members, staff and volunteers on the five teams so they can work together on broad issues.

However you organize, make sure you have these 5 bases covered. The Strategy team can include the chairs of the other 4 groups plus the CEO, or it can be a group unto itself. Again this framework helps ensure that everything important gets covered and that there is a group already in place for every cross-functional or large problem which comes up.

As Albert Einstein said, "Everything should be as simple as possible, but no simpler." The Total Success System™ is just such a solution – about as simple as you can get, but (or should we say therefore) very powerful.

A POWERFUL SYSTEM FOR TOTAL BUSINESS SUCCESS

References:

The Power of Alignment: How Great Companies Stay Centered and Accomplish Extraordinary Things, by George Labovitz and Victor Rosansky:
http://www.amazon.com/exec/obidos/ASIN/0471177903/wwwlciwebcom

The Balanced Scorecard: Translating Strategy Into Action, by Robert Kaplan and David Norton:
http://www.amazon.com/exec/obidos/ASIN/0875846513/wwwlciwebcom

Want professional help to increase your company's success?
Contact the author of this e-book, Buck Lawrimore, through his website:
http://www.Lciweb.com

Made in the USA
Lexington, KY
20 September 2015